IN SEARCH OF GOLD MOUNTAIN

THE CHINESE EXPERIENCE IN 19TH CENTURY AMERICA

MARGARET LAPLANTE

Other books by the same author include:

The DeAutremont Brothers: America's Last Great
Train Robbery

On To Oregon: The Stories Of Seventy Families
Who Settled In The Rogue Valley

Murdered In The Line Of Duty: Constable George Prescott

Images Of America: Jacksonville, Oregon

The books are available at roguecrime.com

In Search Of Gold Mountain
Margaret LaPlante
Copyright 2010 Margaret LaPlante

Printed in the United States of America

ISBN: 978-1456426002

CHAPTER I – THE EARLY YEARS

It was as if the word GOLD echoed around the world as people came to the Pacific Northwest in droves in search of sudden wealth in the 1850s. Most of the newcomers were white men from every corner of the globe but there was another group of immigrants who traveled just as far seeking their fortune. They were called Celestials or Sojourners, but neither term was spoken in a positive manner. They were the Chinese. They traveled far in search of Gum Shan, also known as Gold Mountain. Lured to America dreaming of the wealth that had eluded them in their native land, they came by the thousands. They arrived on American soil, not with the intent of beginning a new life here, but instead to work the gold fields then return home with enough money to be able to provide for their families.

News of the discovery of gold in California reached China by way of British and American trading vessels. This was welcome news to young men living in the Kwangtung Province (known today as Canton.) Kwangtung's lowlands were home to the fertile Delta of the Pearl River. This area had been China's rice basket for thousands of years. About the time the American West was expanding, China's rice basket was experiencing problems of its own. The Pearl River Delta was no stranger to the wrath of Mother Nature. Typhoons and floods would wipe out a year's crop. This could be followed by years of drought and famine.

Family farms had been divided by each generation as was their tradition. By the mid 1800s many of the Chinese found they did not have enough land to support their family. Poor living conditions and civil strife engulfed China during this time. Floods wiped out the crops in 1847-1848. This was followed by the Taiping Rebellion that began in 1851. At heart was the desire to not be under the Manchu rule and the need for land reform. The warfare continued for more than a decade with an estimated cost of 20,000 lives lost before the Manchu armies crushed their opponents declaring victory in 1864.

The 1860s brought no relief. The new decade ushered in conflict between ethnic groups and competing clans in southern Kwangtung. The competition was fierce for land that would produce the crops they so desperately needed. Those who had been in the Pearl River Delta the longest (known as Punti) felt strongly that any new comers (known as Hakka) were not entitled to any land. The result was a war between the Punti and Hakka that dragged on for years and even carried over once they were on American soil.

The opportunities that awaited the Chinese in America provided welcome relief from the strife at home. The long journey to a foreign land rife with uncertainties looked much more promising than the reality of staying put. As one Chinese farmer said, "I work on four-mou land [less than one acre, a larger-than-average holding] year in and year out, from dawn to dusk, but after taxes and providing for your own needs, I make $20 a year. You make that much in one day. No matter how much it cost to get there, or how hard the work is, America is still better than this."

The majority of Chinese immigrants were young men who travelled alone, leaving their wives and children behind. This was no easy journey. For those who set out in the 1850s, they traveled by sailing ships that could take three months or more at sea. The 1860s saw the advent of the Trans-Pacific steamship which shortened the time to approximately 45 days. Either way the journey was excruciatingly difficult. The men were crammed into close quarters for the long and arduous journey. The fare to America was about fifty dollars. However, that price could be doubled or tripled and the interest rate could be unscrupulous. Those without the means to pay for their fare up front, could enlist with one of six Associations based in China. The Associations would pay for their travel. Once they arrived on American soil, they were met by a China boss who worked for the Association. The men had no option but to go to work for their new China boss in order to repay their debt. The men knew their families back home could be in grave danger if they failed to repay their debt to the Association.

The China boss would decide where to send the new arrivals based on what contracts he had from the white miners. In the beginning the China bosses took the new arrivals to mining camps in California. These were exciting times in California. No sooner had one mining camp sprung up than gold was discovered nearby. Over time the Chinese pushed forward into other territories of the Pacific Northwest and eventually to all of America. What began as a trickle of Chinese leaving the Celestial Empire grew to a huge exodus.

Auburn, California   California State Library

The gold rush town of Yreka, California in the 1850s
Photo courtesy of Siskiyou County Museum, Yreka,
California

China Row in Yreka, California
Photo courtesy of Siskiyou County Museum, Yreka,
California

A typical pioneer log cabin that housed white settlers
Photo courtesy of Siskiyou County Museum, Yreka,
California

CHAPTER II – THE LIFESTYLE

The Chinese kept to themselves and honored the customs of their homeland. This created distrust amongst the white men for the Chinese. They ridiculed the Chinese for their manner of dress and their customs.

The Chinese generally ignored the whites but no town was immune from the fighting that broke out between the opposing parties. The Chinese were usually on the losing end of these battles. Murders took place and even if the Chinese were not to blame, they frequently found themselves on the wrong side of the law. This is not to say the Chinese were innocent bystanders for they certainly did their fair share of fighting. However, they were generally not the instigators. The feuds were usually about their willingness to work for lower wages and thus taking jobs from the whites. However, the whites did not fight the China bosses, the very people who negotiated the contracts.

Typical dress for the Chinese men was a skull cap, a long thin blue coat, thin blue cotton pants, white stockings and shoes that were far from sturdy. As time went by, many cast aside their flimsy cotton shoes for a pair of sturdy boots. Some adopted the American brimmed hat made from felt. The Chinese women who came to America during this time adorned their hair with a ribbon or an artificial flower, they carried fans and wore basic long cotton blouses over matching trousers. Children were dressed lavishly for celebrations but otherwise wore basic attire.

Chinese men kept their hair in a queue (long hair in the back.) Returning to China with short hair could result in death at the hands of Chinese authorities. There were legal cases in America where the punishment was for a man's hair to be cut drastically short, knowing how devastating that was to the Chinese. Some jails would cut the hair of any male imprisoned to one inch, knowing doing so could bring great anguish to any Chinese male.

Due to the transitory nature of their work, most of the Chinese miners lived in tents initially. If it appeared there would be enough work in an area, the tents gave way to wooden structures. These structures were generally just crude buildings set on rocks or blocks of wood. The wind howled through the thin walls and the rain poured down, yet the men were content and grateful for the shelter. The structures were generally attached to one another, creating "China Rows" as they were called.

For those wanting to stay current on the news from home, they could purchase a newspaper printed in San Francisco and distributed to stores in the rural areas that requested a copy. It was important to the Chinese to stay in touch with their families back home. For those who could neither read nor write, they asked one of their brethren to complete the task for them. The Associations made sure the letters were delivered to China via one of the trading vessels.

Although there was a large population of Chinese in the Pacific Northwest, most lived in rural areas where there were few if any stores where they could obtain Chinese provisions. Some stores welcomed the Chinese and kept a supply of goods just for them. In other areas a Chinese man would open a store to stock food items, clothing and necessities for his countrymen. Some towns prohibited the Chinese from operating a mercantile. If need be, the China bosses would order supplies from shops in San Francisco or Portland. This only added to the ire of the white men as they felt the Chinese were not willing to spend their money in their own community. They looked upon this as a way for the Chinese to avoid supporting the local economy.

If a white settler did open his doors to the Chinese, he risked being ostracized by his fellow European settlers. Kasper Kubli, who hailed from Switzerland, welcomed the Chinese to his store in the Applegate area of Southern Oregon. A glance through the ledgers of Mr. Kubli's store shows that from 1864-1865 he served more than one hundred Chinese miners who were employed in nearby placer mining operations. Mr. Kubli ordered merchandise from Tung Chong and Company in San Francisco. In 1865 Wanng Tonm, a miner, purchased oil for 75¢, nails for 25¢, a shovel for $1.62, salt for 50¢, beans for 25¢, sugar for 25¢, whiskey for 62¢, tobacco for 50¢, butter for $1, garlic for 25¢, matches for 75¢, 1 pair of boots for $5.75, 2 pairs of pants for $4, a shirt for $1 and a hat for $3.75. This would indicate Wanng Tonm was transitioning his native clothing for sturdier clothing similar to what the white men were wearing. This was probably done in an effort to stay warm and dry rather than assimilating to the western life.

Common items purchased by the Chinese from Mr. Kubli included:

Tea, soy sauce, spices such as ginger and cinnamon, oysters, sardines, black beans, dried shrimp, bamboo shoots, dry cabbage and other dried vegetables, salt pork, bacon, flour, salt, sugar and oil.

The eating habits of those from Asia were yet another source of amusement for the white settlers. They could not fathom how the Chinese existed on such little food. Generally within the Chinese mining camps there was one person who did the cooking. Each evening they would gather in groups and sit on rocks in front of small black pots that were heated by fire. Their main staple was rice, supplemented by vegetables and a protein. The protein could be vermin, small animals, chicken or pork.

In comparison the whites choose coffee as their beverage, red meat whenever possible, flour, sugar, salt, lard, bacon and butter. The men hunted and fished to supplement the food available at the merchantiles. As for their wardrobe, they generally wore Levi's, flannel shirts, western boots, coats, hats and gloves.

The expense of importing rice in the mid 19th century had many Chinese turning to flour and any type of rising agent they could find to make a steamed bun. Another item that had to be imported was tea. The cost of this necessity ranged from 50¢-75¢ per pound.

Depending on their location, some of the Chinese were able to put their native fishing skills to use to supplement the fowl and pork they consumed. They were not known for eating red meat; however there are recorded instances of that occurring. This may have been out of necessity rather than by choice.

Whenever possible, the Chinese planted gardens to supplement their food supply. They had been farmers at home so this came quite naturally to them. Some of the Chinese were able to make a living at raising vegetables, thereby forgoing the work of a miner.

Another aspect missing from many rural areas was a place for the Chinese to worship. Whenever possible, the Chinese would build a place of worship known as a Joss House. The Joss House was very important to the Chinese as it served as not only a place to worship but also as a community center.

There were secret societies amongst the Chinese known as Tongs. They were more common in the cities than in the country. The initial purpose of the Tong was to offer the Chinese protection from those who tried to take advantage of them. In reality the tongs were known for gambling, promoting prostitution, and fighting other tongs.

There were occasional marriages and births amongst the Chinese. One birth was recorded in the Jacksonville, Oregon newspaper, the *Democratic Times*, on August 13, 1868 wherein the paper reported: "A young Celestial may excite some curiosity now… after awhile we will become more used to the animal."

Most women stayed in China and waited for the men to return home. Many of the female gender who ventured to the new country were "big footed" meaning their feet were not bound. Such an abnormality made them most undesirable. Faced with cultural discrimination, most of these women worked as prostitutes. They served both the white men and the Chinese. The women who did accompany their husbands to America formed a tight knit community. They spent their time inside the home, rarely venturing out. When they were seen in public, they were met with stares and sometimes cruel comments due to their bound feet.

For more than one thousand years young girls between the ages of three and eleven were expected to have their feet bound. Known as "lily feet," they were thought to be a symbol of gentility and high class. Women who did not have bound feet were destined to a life working in the fields or as prostitutes. The actual practice of binding the foot consisted of pressing the toes under the foot. The arches were then broken as the foot was pulled straight with the leg and the foot was wrapped very tightly in a cotton bandage that held the toes underneath the foot. After a period of two-three years the feet were so badly deformed the girl could fit into the much coveted "Lotus shoes." By this time the toes were so badly deformed that sometimes they fell off due to the lack of blood circulation. This process was extremely painful and walking was excruciatingly difficult. The result was the women were kept in seclusion at home and did not venture out often. One Chinese lady with bound feet recalled her personal struggle when she had to flee her home in San Francisco's Chinatown following the earthquake and fire in 1906. She had never been far from home and found herself having to find a safe haven. In the end a white man helped her reach a safe place on the outskirts of town. In 1911 the practice of binding a female's foot was outlawed when the Manchu Dynasty was toppled.

In 1870 a man living in Nevada reported:

> "I regret that it is not in my power to speak more favorably of the female portion of this peculiar people. I am, however, constrained to state that by universal consent, they are avowed without almost a solitary exception to have professionally bartered away the brightest jewel of a virtuous women."

The Chinese were known for was their use of opium. This carried over once they arrived in America. The drug was carried on the ships and made available to the immigrants through stores in San Francisco. It didn't take long for the white settlers to take a severe dislike to this habit. Newspapers in San Francisco carried stories complaining about the opium dens frequented by Chinese males. However, it was not just in the cities, the miners in rural areas used the drug just as voraciously. There were no laws prohibiting the use of the narcotic. Many of the Chinese also used tobacco. They used plug or loose tobacco which they placed in pipes and smoked. Alcohol also played a role in the lives of the Chinese. Some enjoyed a spirit or wine with their evening meal. In cities men were frequently seen in a stupor from the opium but in the rural areas they may have known their limits for there weren't many accounts of the men just lying around. Even their harshest critics had to admit neither the opium, nor the alcohol, prevented the Chinese from working hard at any given job.

It could be said that the Chinese loved a celebration. To honor the customs of their native homeland, they celebrated Chinese New Year with great enthusiasm. Whether they lived in a city or in a rural area, everyone participated in the celebration. No celebration was complete without firecrackers which they ordered from Chinese stores in the larger cities. Early on the morning of Chinese New Year, the Chinese dressed in new (or freshly laundered) clothing. They visited their Joss House if there was one nearby. If there were females and children present, the women would dress the children in new clothing they made by hand for the celebration. The children would then go door to door receiving candy (sometimes the white children were invited to participate in this activity.) In some areas the Chinese also gave out white lilies. The houses along China Row were adorned with red pieces of paper that held words of happiness and hope for a good year. Generally a parade was held and afterward games were played. Feasts of food were enjoyed and shared with other Chinese. At night they would light red lanterns and play musical instruments including drums and cymbals.

In what might be described as a vicious circle, the treatment bestowed on the Chinese, led to exactly what the whites ridiculed them for. They did not assimilate to American culture but instead chose to honor the customs and beliefs of their native land. This behavior kept them at bay with the whites and led to distrust and missed opportunities for each to learn from the other.

Chinese man in a photography studio in Helena, Montana
Montana Historical Society

A Chinese man in a photography studio in Walla, Walla Washington

Ty Hang   Fort Benton, Montana

Chinese in Arizona

Chinese child in Arizona

Soo Ling Virginia City, Montana.   Montana Historical Society

Chinese women walking on bound feet

A Chinese woman in a photography studio

Photo courtesy of Siskiyou County Museum, Yreka,
California

Photo courtesy of Siskiyou County Museum, Yreka, California

A Chinese man in a photography studio
Idaho State Historical Society

San Francisco, California Chinatown

Chinese children Salem, Oregon

Chinese children in California
California Historical Society

San Francisco, California Chinatown

Early day mining camp

Chinatown LaGrande, Oregon

Chinese Joss House

Interior of a Joss House in Yreka, California
Photo courtesy of Siskiyou County Museum, Yreka,
California

Chinese Lunar New Year Celebration Centerville, Idaho

A Chinese Celebration
California Historical Society

A Chinese New Year's Day parade in Yreka, California
Photo courtesy of Siskiyou County Museum, Yreka,
California

Chinese New Year celebration in Etna, California with
firecrackers in the background
Photo courtesy of Siskiyou County Museum, Yreka,
California

A Chinese man lighting a firecracker during a celebration in Yreka, California

Photo courtesy of Siskiyou County Museum, Yreka, California

CHAPTER III – THE WORK

It was the allure of gold that initially brought the Chinese to America. However, once they arrived in this new country they found many obstacles blocking their dreams of striking it rich in the gold fields. For starters the Chinese were not allowed to own mining claims. Once a white man abandoned the mining claim, a Chinese man could work it as his own. There were many instances where a white settler had given up on the claim, only to learn later a Chinese man had struck it rich. Most sought their own revenge, others sought the help of the court system. However, since the Chinese were not allowed to testify against a white man, the legal system served little purpose for them.

Some of the white miners sold their mining claim as they moved to another location. An example of such a transaction dated August 20, 1859 from Wolf Creek, Oregon read:

> "Know all men by those present that I the undersigned have this day sold 1 mining claim 150 yards together with 8 sluice boxes, 2 picks, 2 shovels, 2 hatchets, 1 root ax and 1 cabin to 1 Chinaman by the name of Chick, for the sum of 30 dollars. Ephraim Allen. Paid cash 4 dollars, the other 26 to be paid in 5 days."

Some Chinese remained in San Francisco forgoing the lure of the gold fields. Instead they tried their hand at life in the city. Those who had the means operated businesses such as wash houses, restaurants or stores.

Another occupation for the Chinese male was to be a servant for a white family either in the city or in a rural area. Some of the families embraced their new hire and over time grew quite fond of him. The work of a servant could be difficult but it provided a certain stability that was lacking in the transitory nature of gold mining.

There were a number of Chinese laundries throughout the Pacific Northwest. One Chinese male could operate the business with little overhead. That was until certain communities began to tax the Chinese heavily for operating such businesses while at the same time, not taxing their white counterparts. In 1883 Ashland, Oregon, passed an ordinance that taxed a Chinese washhouse or laundry forty dollars per year. In nearby Jacksonville, Oregon, there was an ordinance that read: "Every person who shall set up or keep a business, any washhouse or laundry, shall pay a quarterly license tax of no less than five dollars." In addition to the taxes, some of the Chinese wash houses met with violence. In Anaconda, Montana, a Chinese laundry was bombed in 1890. In 1893 Wing Lee operated a laundry in Grants Pass, Oregon. He lived on the property with three other Chinese men. During the early morning hours of October 17th someone tried to blow up the building. The men escaped unharmed but the message came through loud and clear.

Once the "easy" gold had been panned out of the rivers and streams in California and Oregon the China bosses looked for other methods to extract the gold from the land. The

1860s saw the beginning of placer mining. Placer mining was first developed in California then made its way to other states. Placer mining involved bringing in huge pieces of hydraulic machinery at great expense. The machinery was used to blast away at the walls of a canyon thus freeing any gold. The China bosses hired out their men to work in hydraulic mining ventures owned by companies operated by white men. There were instances of China bosses running their own hydraulic mining operations but this was rare.

Some of the Chinese went to work in the agriculture industry clearing the land for planting. Others found work in canneries, packing houses, clearing roads for stagecoaches, building rock walls or farming.

As early as the 1860s, many of the Chinese went to work building railroads. As the western United States expanded, there was a need to link one area of the country to another. For more than twenty years thousands of Chinese men made their living building the railroads we still use today. When they finished one railroad line, they began work on another.

This new career could have meant a new beginning, but the discrimination followed them. The China Bosses secured contracts to provide labor at much lower rates than what the whites were earning which only added fuel to the fire. For example, on one railroad line the Chinese were paid twenty-eight dollars per month for their labor. In comparison the white workers received thirty-five dollars per month plus room and board. There was a time in Washington State the Chinese went on strike demanding the same wages the whites received. Their voices were lost amongst their bosses and they never received more money.

Work on the railroads proved excruciatingly hard. When one railroad executive of the Central Pacific Railroad questioned if the Chinese would be physically able to perform the work, one of his partners reminded him the Chinese had built the Great Wall of China so surely they could build a few railroads. The Chinese laborers proved him right by working long, hard hours.

Across New Mexico and Arizona the Chinese helped build railroads through the dessert in harsh weather conditions. In Northern California the stretch of railroad over the Siskiyou Mountains proved to be excruciating. More than 4,000 workers spent years laying tracks and building tunnels through the mountains that were covered in snow more than half the year. The mountains of the Sierra Nevada in California proved equally troublesome due to the weather and steep, mountainous terrain. In one location the terrain rose 7,000 feet in just one hundred miles. It was necessary to blast into the mountain with dynamite. At times, the workers had to be lowered in baskets so they could chip away at the granite and plant the dynamite in the mountain.

As they dug, blasted and shoveled their way inch by inch, the Chinese did so without complaining. The work was treacherous and for many their journey ended at the railroad. They met their death due to the dangerous work.

After work on the railroad ended, the Chinese looked for other ways to make a living. In Wyoming and other states thousands of Chinese found work in the coal mines. The following agreement is between the China bosses who provided the labor and Union Pacific Railroad who owned the mines.

"Agreement made and entered into, this 24th day of December A.D. 1875, between Beckwith, Quinn & Co., of Evanston, Wyoming Territory of the first part, and the Union Pacific Railroad Co., of the Second part,- Witnesseth: -

The parties of the first part, hereby agree to furnish to the party of the Second part, all the Chinese laborers requisite for the complete working of their several Coal mines on the line of the Union Pacific Railroad, at the same prices and on the same terms and conditions as stated in a certain Contract for similar service made by Sisson Wallace & Co., for an in behalf of Chinese laborers, with the Rocky Mountain Coal & Mining Co., a copy of which is hereto attached, and made part of this agreement.

The said parties of the first part further agree to furnish to the said party of the Second part, upon a reasonable notice from their General Superintendent, a sufficient number of Chinese laborers for the repairs of the track of the Union Pacific Railroad, or such portion thereof, in addition to that which is now being worked by Chinamen, as the party of the Second part may require . . . .

Chinamen agree to mine the coal, load it in Pit cars, and deliver it at the mouth of the room free from slack and rock, and assorted, either lump, small or mixed as directed, at Seventy Four (74) cents coin per ton of Twenty Two hundred and Forth (2240) pounds, from all places, either rooms, levels of air courses.

All cars of coal sent out of the mine in which there is slack or rock, will be docked half of their weight, and if men disobey their Foreman, or persist in sending out slack or rock, after being docked, they will be discharged.

All men are to commence and stop work by the whistle.

Company are to furnish tools, do the blacksmithing and repairing, furnish mules, harness and pit cars, and supply of water for the men.

Company are to deliver coal at the houses of all the laborers, for which the Chinamen are to pay 50 Cents per man per month.

Company are to furnish houses for the Chinamen to live in at $5, per month for each house."

Shortly before the 19th century drew to a close, many Chinese found themselves once again traveling in search of gold. This time it was to the newly discovered gold mines in Alaska. For some the dream of striking it rich finally came true, for others the dream ended when the last American Gold Rush came to an end high in the hills of Alaska.

Sung Lung Washing & Ironing House Salem, OR

Building the Central Pacific Railroad in Utah

Schafer Brothers Logging Company

Schafer Brothers Lumber Company

Pacific National Lumber Company

Hydraulic mining in California

Grading a railroad in northern California
Photo courtesy of Siskiyou County Museum Yreka,
California

The dangerous work of building a railroad into a mountain

San Francisco Chinatown
California Historical Society

Some of the Chinese carried items in baskets on poles.
There were instances of towns passing laws prohibiting
anyone from carrying such contraptions on sidewalks,
thereby forcing the Chinese to walk in the streets.
Photo courtesy of Siskiyou County Museum Yreka,
California

CHAPTER IV – ANTI CHINESE

It did not take long before hostility and violence against the Chinese grew to epic proportions in California as more and more Chinese arrived. The San Francisco Custom House recorded 2,716 Chinese arrivals in 1851. The following year they recorded 20,000 arrivals from China. In 1852 California's Governor, John Bilger, who at first had admired the Chinese, became an outspoken opponent. He declared the Chinese "were a menace." This only served to cement the feelings of the whites and tensions ran high in every community in the state.

From the journal of a white settler in 1852:

"Chinamen are getting to be altogether too plentiful in the country. Pard and I chased a dozen off of our river claims and warned them that we would shoot them if we found them there again. We called a miners meeting and adopted a miners' law that they should not be allowed to take up or hold ground for themselves. Some were for driving them out of the country entirely, but the majority thought it would be good to sell them claims, as it was an easy way to make money. They are not looked at as human beings and have no rights that a white man is bound to respect."

There was an instance in Nevada City, California, where a Chinese man was hanged for stealing a mule. Soon after the owner of the mule arrived and announced it was all a mistake. In Butte, Montana a white man hanged a Chinese man after observing him enjoying a successful day working a gold claim.   One white man in Arizona who worked alongside the Chinese building railroads summed it up by saying, "If occasionally a few were killed, no questions were asked and work went on as usual."

The elections of 1870 brought the Chinese into the spotlight. Headlines in San Francisco declared, "The Chinese question is assuming more dangerous proportions every day and threatens to overwhelm the Pacific Coast." In Oregon at the Democratic State Convention of 1876 it was decided, "Resolved: that the large influx of Chinese Immigration to the Pacific Coast has been a curse to the country. (We) pledge ourselves for adoption of such measures as will prevent and cure this growing evil." In 1880 the Governor of California declared March 4th a legal holiday for the locals to participate in anti-Chinese demonstrations.

The day finally came when those in power passed the Chinese Exclusion Act of 1882. Although some Chinese found ways around this law, for the most part it ended the great exodus of Chinese to America. The officials claimed it would limit the competition for jobs. The Exclusion Act was to last ten years but in 1892 it was extended. Additionally, in 1888 the Scott Act was passed which prohibited any Chinese person from re-entering America once he/she left.

The railroad work came to a close across the Pacific Northwest in the mid 1880s during a time America's economy was faltering. There were few job opportunities which only increased the tensions between the Chinese and their critics.

In Seattle, Washington, a labor union known as the Knights of Labor, took to task the capitalists, bankers and railroad companies who they blamed for allowing the Chinese to take jobs away from the whites. They also voiced their displeasure with those in charge of upholding the Exclusion Act of 1882. They felt the officials were too lax, thus allowing more Chinese to arrive on American soil.

In Wyoming in 1885 a group of white miners led by the Knights of Labor attacked a group of Chinese men resulting in twenty-eight deaths and at least fifteen Chinese men being injured. Known as the "Rock Springs Massacre" it was the result of a competition between the two groups over a contract with the Union Pacific Railroad's coal mining industry.

The violence did not stop there. In September of 1885 in Washington state three Chinese hop-pickers died when whites set their barracks on fire near present day Issaquah. Days later in Newcastle, Washington thirty-six coal miners died when their barracks were set on fire. Both attacks were led by the Knights of Labor.

In Tacoma, Washington one newspaper questioned, "Why permit an army of leprous, prosperity-sucking, progress-blasting Asiatics befoul our thoroughfares, degrade the city, repel immigration, drive out our people, break up our homes, take employment from our countrymen, corrupt the morals of our youth, establish opium joints, buy or steal the babe of poverty or slave, and taint with their brothels the lives of our young men? If no other method of keeping them at a distance from our people can be found, let the citizens furnish them with lots on the waterfront, three fathoms below low tide."

In October of 1885 the officials in Tacoma announced that all Chinese would have to leave by the end of the month. Some of the Chinese did obey the order but others chose to stay put. Those who were still in Tacoma at the beginning of November found themselves face-to-face with an angry mob of whites led by Tacoma's mayor and supported by the city police. They invaded Tacoma's Chinatown and ordered its residents out of the city. The Chinese were marched to a railroad depot and put aboard a train to Portland. Within days one would have been hard pressed to know there had ever been a Chinatown in Tacoma. The officials burned the homes and any possessions the Chinese had left behind. The leaders of the mob were indicted and transported to Vancouver, Washington. The judge there set them free on bail. Upon arrival back home in Tacoma they were met with a heros' welcome. The indictments were later dropped.

Not far from Tacoma a boycott was declared in the Seattle, Washington area. The boycott was against any business operated by the Chinese and/or any business that employed the Chinese. Some businesses went so far as to advertise that they did not employ any Chinese. Early in 1886 the officials in Seattle ordered all Chinese to leave the city. Similar to what happened in Tacoma, some left but several hundred stayed behind. On February 7th an angry mob arrived in Seattle's Chinatown and attempted to march all of the Chinese to a waiting steamer ship. Their attempt proved unsuccessful. Surprisingly some of the whites spoke out against the plan. They wanted the Chinese gone, but they wanted to find a way to do so legally. They were concerned about the repercussions if they forced them out. They worried about future business dealings with businesses back east that might look unfavorably upon such actions. Time went by but nothing was resolved. The next attempt to remove the Chinese resulted in the killing of one white and four whites being injured. Based on this, it was decided that every Chinese person had to vacate Seattle. Within a few weeks that became the reality and Seattle took on a new look. After the devastating fire of 1889, many Chinese returned to a newly rebuilt Seattle.

In March of 1886 a large angry mob demanded all Chinese people vacate the city of Portland, Oregon. In Portland it was not just the white men who wanted the Chinese expelled, it was the white women as well. They felt the Chinese were taking work away from them in factories, mills, restaurants and as domestic help. Unlike the other expulsions, this one was never carried out due to the outspoken city officials and local police who worried about the reputation of the city if the plan was carried out.

In 1887 four white men robbed, murdered and mutilated thirty-one Chinese men in the Hell's Canyon region of the Snake River area of Oregon. Three of the white men were brought to trial but were soon acquitted.

Newspapers throughout the Pacific Northwest carried stories and opinions about the Chinese. A few examples include:

"They do not come here to make their homes, they bring no families with them, not even their bones are left here…we are flooded by these Chinese, they impoverish our country, aggrandize themselves and rob our country."

"But the Chinese immigration must be stopped, or they must adopt a style of life that is not offensive to the refined American taste. Let them remain in their own land or conform somewhat to the customs of the people among whom they chose to reside."

"The majority of them lead a very unproductive life. Is this Chinese immigration desirable? I think not. In what capacity do they contribute to the advancement of American interests? Are they engaged in anything that contributes to the general wealth and importance of the country? Will they discard their clannish prepossessions, assimilate with us, buy of us and respect us?"

An article that ran in the *Oregon Sentinel*, on September 1, 1866, summarized the feelings of many of the white settlers who never accepted the Chinese in the community:

"We hope that during the present legislative session, the very important questions of taxing the Chinese miners will not be overlooked. It seems an unwise policy to allow a race of brutish heathens who have nothing in common with us, to exhaust our mineral lands without paying a heavy tax for their occupation. These people bring nothing with them to our shores, they add nothing to the permanent wealth of this country, and so strong is their attachment to their own country they will not let their filthy carcasses lie in our soil. Could these people be taxed to exclude them entirely, it would be a blessing."

On July 10, 1869 the *Democratic Times* of Jacksonville, Oregon reported:

"We do not like to see any species of injustice tolerated in this professed Christian land, even to the lowest and most degraded of God's creatures. It is with candid sincerity, therefore that we protest against the vicious boys of this town being allowed to stone Chinamen when the latter are civilly behaving themselves. In some instances they do not stop with maltreating Chinamen, but are insufferably insulting to white people."

On May 7, 1879, the *Oregon Sentinel* reported, "The Chinese must go. Last week two of our enterprising Chinese having heard of the pure water of Ashland went to that town to start a wash house. They didn't start it however, but started back to Jacksonville just ahead of a yelling crowd of men and boys who heard they had come to break ground for a Joss Temple in that pious city. Pursued by the angry crowd, the heathen missionaries struck into a rapid trot dropping bars of soap and other paraphernalia of their calling as they went."

Feelings ran deep in Salem, Oregon, as well as indicated in an ad in their local newspaper stating, "We are doing more in our little old way to bring this Chinese question to a focus than all the exclusion acts put together, for the surest way to beat the Chinaman is by not giving him an opportunity, or in other words, stop his supplies, shut him off short and he must surely go flee, get your laundry work done by white people. Henderson & Isaacs, agents Salem Steam Laundry."

In 1879 a local newspaper in Arizona referred to the Chinese as, "ignorant, filthy, leprous horde." A few years later another newspaper in Arizona referred to those born in China as, "The most pernicious and degraded race on the globe." Fifteen years after the first article appeared it became obvious the perception had not changed when an Arizona newspaper reported the Chinese were, "A fungus that lives in isolation, sucking the sap of the other plants." In Tucson some of the Chinese worked as farmers. The locals brought a lawsuit claiming they were taking more than their fair share of the water. The Chinese prevailed in the legal proceedings. Soon after the city of Tucson took on a new look with the opening of several Chinese businesses. In 1893 the City Council moved that all Chinese businesses be segregated to one side of town. Their proposal was defeated and the Chinese were allowed to conduct their businesses anywhere within the city.

If the Chinese hoped the discrimination would not follow them as they pushed outward to other states, they were sorely mistaken. In Butte, Montana, the local newspaper, *The Daily Miner*, stated, "A Chinaman could no more become an American citizen than a coyote."

As labor unions in Montana gained strength in the 1880-1890s they organized boycotts to evict Chinese businesses. It got to the point that during the winter of 1896-1897 union members blocked doorways to prevent customers from entering the businesses owned by the Chinese.

Three Chinese businessmen in Butte decided they had had enough. They protested to the United States government and the Chinese government. Garnering no response, they filed a lawsuit against the leaders of the boycotts. The men eventually won the lawsuit but were never able to collect on it. They did receive their legal fees totaling just over $1,700.

In 1897 one Chinese man summed up his feelings by writing:

> "I came to America to labor, to suffer, floating from one place to another, persecuted by the whites for more than twenty years. What is my goal for enduring this kind of pain and hardship? Nothing but trying to earn some money to relieve the poverty of my home. Do you know that both the old and young at my home are awaiting me to deliver them out of starvation and cold?"

In 1904 the Chinese Exclusion Act was extended indefinitely. At the same time the officials passed a law requiring all Chinese to carry identification with a photograph. They also passed a law denying the Chinese the right to writs of *habeas corpus* if arrested. The following year in China, the Chinese declared a boycott of American goods based on how the Chinese were being treated in America. Although this gave the Chinese living in the United States great joy, nothing came of the boycott. The Exclusion Act was finally repealed in 1943. .

Poster from Tacoma, Washington

Poster from Seattle, Washington emphasizing "No Chinamen Employed"

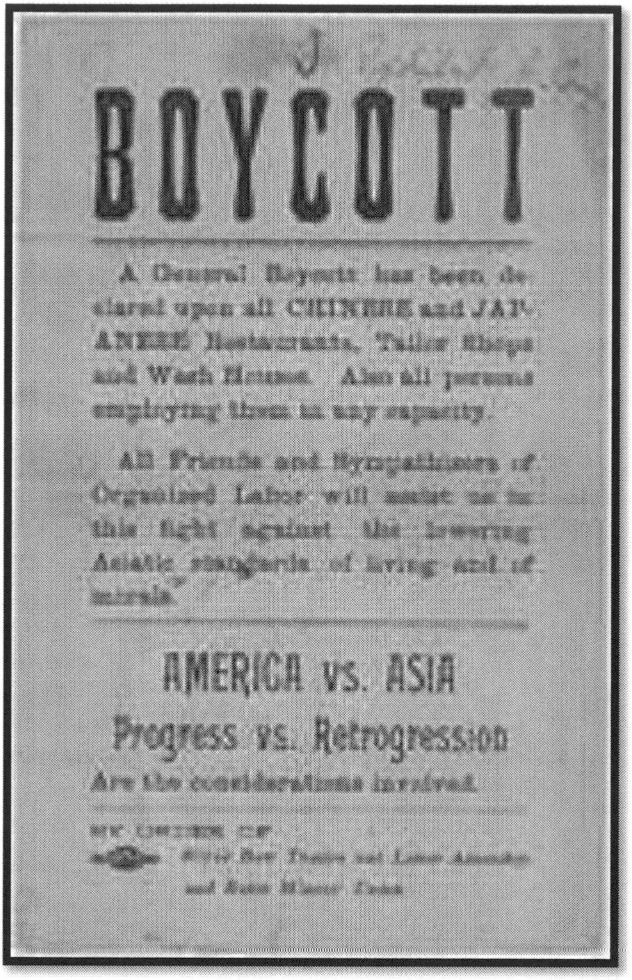

A poster announcing the boycott

Identification as required by law after
the Exclusion Act was passed

CHAPTER V – THE JOURNEY HOME

For some of the Chinese their dreams of returning home, a wealthy man, were never realized. The men died here in America before they found their Gold Mountain. Due to the dangerous work they were engaged in, be it mining or blasting through mountains to build the railroads and tunnels, many succumbed. Disease and illness claimed the lives of others.

The Chinese had burial customs that needed to be adhered to in order to give their loved one a proper burial. The mourners dressed in long white gowns. As the funeral procession left for the cemetery, females would walk out in front and wail loudly. As the possession reached the cemetery slips of fake money were tossed along the route. Upon reaching the burial site, feasts of food were laid out. The feast generally consisted of pork or chicken, fruits, vegetables and breads. Sometimes the clothing of the deceased was laid out as well. The reason for this is they did not want the deceased to go to their next life and be without money, food or clothing. Depending on the community, these items were then burned. Some cemeteries still have remnants of the fire pits used for such occasions. If the cemetery did not have a fire pit, the mourners simply lit the items on fire. In other communities they did not burn the items. Instead they left the items behind. When acts of thievery were reported, the Chinese began taking the items with them when they left the cemetery.

In Jacksonville, Oregon, the Reverend Moses Williams, minister of the Presbyterian Church, had occasion to observe one burial ceremony that he recorded in his journal on Sunday, April 2, 1865. He wrote: "Studied sermon in the morning. Preached at 11 ½ A.M. After sermon Mr. Hoffman, Mrs. Hoffman and I, seeing a number of Chinese going toward the cemetery to perform various rites of superstition at the graves of their countrymen, we went and witnessed the performances, which were these. Two large hogs were brought roasted whole, spread out flat on their bellies on a portable platform of boards, chickens roasted whole with their heads erected as if alive, bread (raised) in loaves, apples, some sort of alcoholic liquors which were afterwards dribbled out at intervals on the ground near the head of the grave. Wax candles and queer looking tapers about 8" long of the size of a small fixings were used. They all went through certain forms of bowing, waving the hands, bringing them clenched or clasped together to the face, as if praying, then kneeled down on a mat or cloth, spread near the head of the grave, bowed the head close to the ground, usually three times, next dribbled from small cups their whiskey on the ground. Then going through the same bowing and raising of the hands. No one tasted any of the food, through the ceremony of cutting off one ear of the hogs and tip end of one wing of one of the chickens. The apples were then cut up into small pieces of which they ate all, leaving none. After the papers were all burned and Chinese crackers were exploded, the ceremonies ended by carrying all the provisions back to the wagons in which they had come from Jackass Creek, leaving only a few pieces of the bread and the smoking tapers and small wax candles at the graves."

The Chinese firmly believed if you died on foreign soil, your soul would not rest until it was returned to your home land. Therefore it was imperative that if you were buried here in America, your bones be returned home. The six Associations all ensured their members they would provide this as a service. The females and children who died in America remained here unless their families made arrangements for the return of their bones. Throughout the country Chinese morticians came to America to collect the bones of the deceased. The mortician would perform a ceremony wherein he scraped the bones with a special brush using spirits and water, then packed the bones into a small box lined with silk. The Chinese had an idiom, *luo ye gui gen*, or falling leaves return to root. Their belief was the immigrant belonged with their ancestors at home. Another saying, *luo ye sheng gen*, meant falling to the ground, growing roots. This meant if the immigrant did not return home, the new country would become his homeland, thus destroying the continuity of his family. Not all of the Chinese who died here returned home. Various circumstances kept some of the men from ever reaching their final destination.

Some communities had a separate section in the cemetery for the Chinese. An article in the Nevada City, California, newspaper from 1861 demanded the Chinese stop using their cemetery citing their "pagan rituals and exhumation practices." In Folsom, California, the city passed an ordinance prohibiting anyone from being buried within the city. This was directed at the Chinese cemetery that was within the city limits. They were able to reach an agreement wherein those already buried could remain, knowing the bones would be shipped back to China in the future.

Due to the fact that most of the Chinese men were here alone without their family, they were simply buried in a small section of the cemetery without the benefit of a marker or a monument. Whenever possible, the Chinese practiced *feng shui* in the location of the burial plots. They preferred to locate the deceased on a hill or a slope facing a body of water.

The Chinese held two ceremonies during the year relating to the deceased. *Qing Ming* (Pure Brightness) was held during the spring and involved cleaning the graves to show respect. The other festival was *Yulanpen* (Hungry Ghosts) to pacify the spirits who were restless because they had not had a proper burial.

Monument of Hop Lee in the Claggett Cemetery
Marion County, Oregon

A Chinese funeral possession

A Chinese funeral procession

Burning items during a Chinese funeral

The historic Chinese cemetery in Yreka, California
Photo courtesy of Siskiyou County Museum Yreka,
California

A Chinese funeral in Colma, California

CHAPTER VI – A BACKWARDS GLANCE

During their time in America the Chinese contributed greatly to the expansion of the western states. They labored tirelessly in streams lined with gold, then later in placer mining. Some found work as servants, others were employed in restaurants and hotels. For those with an entrepreneurial spirit, they opened stores, restaurants, laundries and other businesses. Others became great farmers and provided their communities with the freshest of fruits and vegetables. The canneries, factories and packing houses of the Pacific Northwest benefitted from their hard work. In later years, some of the men found work in the logging industry. Thousands of Chinese worked to build the railroads we still depend on today. The Chinese brought a unique and colorful perspective to an America that was undergoing many changes during that time.

For those fortunate enough to bring their dream to fruition, they returned home to China bringing prosperity and thus honor to their family in a manner they could not have achieved in their native land. Once back home they held celebrations complete with firecrackers and huge feasts of food. After the celebration decisions had to be made as to how best to spend the money. Many of the returning Chinese invested in additional land for their families. Some built new homes and a limited number invested in business ventures. Not everyone who returned home was wealthy. Some never found their Gold Mountain but were nevertheless happy to return home to their families. Others returned home only to find that they had to turn their hard earned money over to the Chinese government.

The one thing neither the whites nor the Chinese could have foretold was that one hundred years later Americans would be so intrigued by the Chinese who walked this land they would do numerous archeological digs to learn more about their time here. Throughout the country, but with an emphasis on the Pacific Northwest, archaeologists set out to discover all they could about the Chinese who were here during the 19th century. Due to the lack of garbage pickup, most refuse was simply buried in the ground during this time period. Common items found from these digs include pieces of pottery from bowls and other eating vessels, old bottles, animal bones (generally chicken and pig,) Chinese gaming pieces such as fan-tan, ceramic and glass marbles, pieces of opium pipes and tins, fragments of old cans, and pieces of jars. Much of the porcelain located is from a pattern known as "double luck" although some of the pottery is from the "four seasons" pattern. There are also fragments of eating utensils and cooking wares. Some of the digs revealed bits of glass, possibly from kerosene lamps. There are large and small pieces of stoneware that may have been used to hold any number of food related items such as dried fruits, vegetables or condiments.

There is a saying that if we do not learn from history, we are destined to repeat it. Perhaps there is something we can all learn from the Chinese experience in America during the 19th century.

Artifacts from Deadwood, Idaho archeological digs

Above: Pieces of porcelain. Below: Medicine bottles
from Deadwood, Idaho archeological
digs

Currier, Viola Noon. The Chinese Web in Oregon History. Thesis written in 1928 for the University of Oregon.

Dodds, Gordon B. Oregon A Bicentennial History. W.W. Norton and Company, Inc. New York, New York. American Association for state and local history. Nashville, Tennessee. 1977.

Gilmore, Jesse Lee. A History of Rogue River Valley Pioneer Period 1850-1862. Dissertation for the University of California, 1948.

Edited by Lamar, Howard R. The New Encyclopedia of the American West. University Press, New Haven at London.

Farkas, lani Ah Tye. Bury My Bones In America. Carl Mautz Publishing, Nevada City, California, 1998.

Edited by Fessler, Loren W. Chinese In America Stereotyped Past, Changing Present. Complied by China Institute in America, Inc. Vintage Press, 1983.

Choy, Philip P., Dong, Lorraine, Hom, Marlon K. Coming Man 19th Century American Perceptions of the Chinese. University Washington Press, Seattle, Washington, 1994.

Edited by Chan, Sucheng. Entry Denied Exclusion and the Chinese Community in America 1882-1943. Temple University Press, Philadelphia, Pennsylvania 1991.

Penner, Liisa. The Chinese In Astoria, Oregon 1870-1880. A look at local newspaper articles, the census and other related materials. Thesis 1990.

References:

Bancroft, Hubert Howe. History of Oregon Volume I. The History Company Publishers, San Francisco, California. McGraw-Hill Company 1886.

Bancroft, Hubert Howe. History of Oregon 1848-1888 Volume XXX. The History Company Publishers, San Francisco, California. McGraw-Hill Company.

Carey, Charles Henry. History of Oregon Volume I. The Pioneer Historical Publishing Company, 1922.

Gaston, Joseph. The Centennial History of Oregon Volume I 1811-1912. The S.J. Clarke Publishing Company, 1912.

Kwong, Peter and Dusanka, Miscevic. Chinese America. The New Press, New York and London, 2005.

Pfaelzer, Jean. Driven Out: The Forgotten War Against Chinese Americans. Random House, New York, 2002.

Handbury, Joan. The Chinese In The Rogue Valley 1850-1890 Research paper 1980

LaLande, Jeff. Sojourners In The Oregon Siskiyous Oregon State University Thesis 1981

Watson, Sandralea. The Chinese in Siskiyou County, A Glimpse from Yreka. Cultural Heritage Section California State Parks & Recreation June 1978. Edited by Michael Handryx and James T. Rock for the Siskiyou Pioneer Society Yearbook Volume 6, Number 3, 1990.

Chinese Consolidated Benevolent Association. Dreams of the West: A History of the Chinese in Oregon 1850-1950. Ooligan Press, 2007

Idaho State Historical Society Education Series

http://library.thinkquest.org/20619/Chinese.html

http://www.wwcc.cc.wy.us/wyo_hist/1850.htm

http://www.uidaho.edu/LS/AACC/

http://www.butteamerica.com/fareast.htm